A little book of memories

Buckingha

C000001021

Personal memories inspired by The Francis Frith Collection®

THE FRANCIS FRITH COLLECTION

www.francisfrith.com

Based on a book first published in the United Kingdom in 2013 by The Francis Frith Collection®

This edition published exclusively for Bradwell Books in 2013
For trade enquiries see: www.bradwellbooks.com or tel: 0800 834 920
ISBN 978-1-84589-728-4

British Library Cataloguing in Publication Data

A Little Book of Buckinghamshire Memories
Personal Memories inspired by the Francis Frith Collection

The Francis Frith Collection
6 Oakley Business Park,
Wylye Road, Dinton,
Wiltshire SP3 5EU
Tel: +44 (0) 1722 716 376
Email: info@francisfrith.co.uk
www.francisfrith.com

Printed and bound in Malaysia
Contains material sourced from responsibly managed forests

Front Cover: Chalfont St Giles, The Village c1965 C498043p
Frontispiece: Olney, The Mill c1955 O37018

The colour-tinting is for illustrative purposes only, and is not intended to be historically accurate

A little book of Memories – A Dedication

This book has been compiled from a selection of the thousands of personal memories added by visitors to the Frith website and could not have happened without these contributions. We are very grateful to everyone who has taken the time to share their memories in this way. This book is dedicated to everyone who has taken the time to participate in the Frith Memories project.

It is comforting to find so many stories full of human warmth which bring back happy memories of "the good old days". We hope that everyone reading this book will find stories that amuse and fascinate whilst at the same time be reminded of why we feel affection for Britain and what makes us all British.

Francis Frith always expressed the wish that his photographs be made available to as wide an audience as possible and so it is particularly pleasing to me that by creating the Frith web site we have been able to make this nationally important photographic record of Britain available to a worldwide audience. Now, by providing the Share Your Memories feature on the website we are delighted to provide an opportunity for members of the public to record their own stories and to see them published (both on the website and in this book), ensuring that they are shared and not lost or forgotten.

We hope that you too will be motivated to visit our website and add your own memories to this growing treasure trove – helping us to make it an even more comprehensive record of the changes that have taken place in Britain in the last 100 years and a resource that will be valued by generations to come.

John M Buck
Managing Director
www.francisfrith.com

My lovely childhood at Chalfont St Peter

My father owned the Rose and Crown (a Benskins pub) in Chalfont St Peter from 1946 until 1950, when I was a child. In those days there were hardly any cars going through the village, and we children had such a lot of freedom. We would go up to Chalfont Heights and search the hedgerows to pick wild flowers (there were no laws to protect wild flowers then). I don't know if they still grow there but Green Hill Common was covered in harebells in those days. In the autumn we would scrump for apples and pick blackberries and hazelnuts. One of the favourite tricks of us village children in summer was to wade along the Misbourne River under the main road and blow loud raspberries as people walked over the bridge. I must admit it made a lovely loud echo!

Ivy Jones

Chalfont St Peter, High Street c1950   C524007

Life in Castle Street in Aylesbury in the 1950s

My husband, Roger Watts, and his family lived in Castle Street in Aylesbury in the 1950s. On the right of this photograph is a figure standing outside their front door (number 15) which could be his mother or older sister Linda. Roger's house was not only home to his family of six but also had his grandfather and a lodger under the same roof. He slept in an attic room, with access from a ladder on the landing; it was cold in winter and hot in summer, but it gave him the opportunity to drop sprigs of ivy seeds onto the heads of passing neighbours without being noticed – hours of innocent fun! The children in the street attended the local school, St Mary's, including a number of children with Italian fathers, thanks to the number of ex POWs who stayed in the area following the war. Playground language lessons included how to swear in two languages, which if overheard by the headmaster earned a stroke with a cane across the legs – not very PC these days, but post-war children were made of sterner stuff!

Lesley Watts

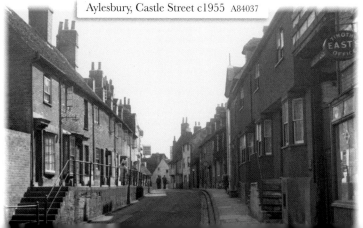

Aylesbury, Castle Street c1955   A84037

3

Happy days at Fenny Stratford

In 1951, when I was about 5, my family moved to Fenny Stratford where we lived with my gran, Mrs Gibson, in Church Street. My two brothers and myself attended the Salvation Army Sunday School nearby, we only lived few doors away and felt grown up walking the few yards to it. I used to play the tambourine there (well, I used to rattle it about a bit). Almost next door to us was our local fire brigade, all the kids used to gather round there when the siren went off on the council offices, knowing lots of men would be running like mad from wherever they worked –

> "Almost next door to us was our local fire brigade, all the kids used to gather round there when the siren went off."

mainly as cooks in the brush factory in Victoria Road. They were all volunteer firemen, bless 'em! My gran was one of the first people around to have a TV, on Coronation Day in 1953 there were people standing in her front room and sitting on her wall at the front with the window open and the sound turned up loud.

Margaret Hogg

Watch your head!

My late sister, Daphne Hemmings, used to own Number 3 Coldharbour Cottage at Wendover. I have fond memories of visiting her there and staying awhile in these fascinating dwellings. You wouldn't want to be six-foot plus with the low doorways plus the low oak beams on the ceilings, you would crack your head on them! If anyone passed away upstairs their body had to be lowered through a trapdoor located in the front bedroom in line with the front door. As a schoolboy during the Second World War years I used to walk from Aylesbury to Wendover up Coombe Hill to the Monument and in the war years (if my memory serves me correct) there were dummy anti-aircraft guns all around the hills.

Peter Osbourne

Wendover, Coldharbour Cottages, Tring Road 1899 44771

Saturday job, kippers and Dr Who in High Wycombe

Many years ago I had a Saturday job in the Woolworth's store in Church Street in High Wycombe (the shop with the large white awning seen in the centre of this photograph), and at the end of the day one of my jobs was to oil the old and dingy wooden floor. I have two golden memories of the store. One is of being asked to turn the boxes of loose biscuits around and date-stamp them again a year hence, as they had already reached their 'best-before' date! The other is of working in the 'cage' where the soft drinks were kept. Being very thirsty on a hot day, I would carefully remove the foil-covered tops from Lucozade bottles, drink the top inch and then carefully replace the tops!

Donald Macdonald

I remember going shopping in High Wycombe with my parents on Saturdays in the 1960s. We'd go to Aldridge's for fruit and vegetables and Brazil's (pronounced 'Brazzles') for pork pies and black pudding. Both shops were on the high street opposite one another. I remember eating cockles on a cocktail stick in a little white saucer – and sometimes shrimps – in the Cornmarket. I remember the toy shop – JS Davy's – on the corner of Queen Victoria Road and Easton Street, and also have fond memories of the Murrays department store, I was always fascinated by the wavy canopy that hung above the front entrance. We went to see Father Christmas there several times. Almost opposite Murrays was a narrow street where we used to get kippers and cod's roe, which we ate on Saturday evening whilst watching 'Doctor Who' and the Daleks on television.

Jayne Smith

High Wycombe, Church Street from the Churchyard c1955　H84068

Stoke Poges – where I grew up

My mum and dad moved into the village of Stoke Poges in the 1930s into a new house in Rogers Lane and lived there for 66 years. My father was the village tailor, working from a workshop in the back garden, and was also a Special Policeman during and just after the Second World War. I was born in 1944 and spent my childhood playing in the fields which surrounded Stoke Poges, of which all but a few have now been built on. I can remember many things from my childhood, including going up to the common and selecting our Christmas tree each year. When they first moved into Stoke Poges Mum and Dad were told they had the rights of the common, and this gave them the right to pick their own pea and bean sticks and a tree. Mum was very much into the history of Stoke Poges, and she later found out that this right came from heathland on the common which had been designated as a 'Poors Fuel Allotment' as a result of an Act of Enclosure in 1810.

Vivien Halse (née Sowersby)

> "My father was the village tailor, working from a workshop in the back garden."

Life at Dinton in the 1940s

I was born (in 1940) and grew up in Dinton, where my Nan ran the public house called the Seven Stars Inn. The pub bar had two rooms, a small lounge and a large bar. Nan served from a small bar in the wall. Dominos was an almost nightly game in the pub and darts were played sometimes. The pub was a very atmospheric old building, it had very narrow stairs to the bedrooms, two small and one very big, which were used to house refugees from London during the Second World War. The Aylesbury Brewery lorry would come every Thursday and the men always had a pint outside before going on. The cellar was right under the front door entrance so was easy to stock into.

> "In those days we had a fish and chip van which visited the village each week, and of course there was a daily milkman."

In those days we had a fish and chip van which visited the village each week, and of course there was a daily milkman. In 1949 Sir Carol Reed filmed 'Daughter of Darkness' in the village in which I was an 'extra', riding on a cart. All the villagers were swanning around like Hollywood stars for a few weeks!

Dennis A Young

Memories of Tinker's End

Around 1975-76 my father, Mr Hugh Jenkins, bought the house on the right of this photograph of Manor Road in Oving, which was called Tinkers End. I lived there until I married a local girl in 1981 and have lived in Aylesbury ever since. Around 1985 my father managed to buy the end cottage as well, and my wife and I used this house as a temporary home for several months, as our own new house was not yet built. The first night I slept in the house was not a good one as I got no sleep, because all night long there was such a noise. In the morning I went looking for the source of this noise and found that it was coming from a sheep in a field about two miles away, across the fields towards Wadderson. I thought the town I came from was more peaceful!

Chris Jenkins

Oving, Manor Road c1955 O118008

Freewheeling down this hill...

I lived at Chalfont St Peter as a young boy in the 1960s. One day me and my friends found an old bike that had no chain and no brakes. We hid the bike in the gorse on the common, and every day after school we'd get the bike out and take it in turns to freewheel down the slope seen in this photograph. Then we'd push it back up and someone else would have a go. I would have been seven at the time.

Donald Macdonald

> "We'd take it in turns to freewheel down the slope seen in this photograph"

Chalfont St Peter, The Common c1955   C524010

Bell ringing at Dorney

The photograph on the opposite page shows the church I was baptised in, the Church of St James the Less at Dorney. As I child in the 1960s I used to go bell ringing here. We had to climb up the very narrow stairwell, being very careful not to slip, and we practiced every week. There were six bells and I rang Number 4. Our teacher would stress to us not to break the stay as it was very expensive to replace so I always felt nervous ringing the bell. Goodness knows what it must have sounded like when we were learning, as all of Dorney Reach and Dorney village would have heard us.

Monica Peck

Playing on the machinery and dodging cows in Fenny Stratford

I lived in Fenny Stratford as a child in the 1950s. At the end of Staple Hall Road, just down from where we lived, was a council yard where some heavy machinery was stored, mainly a very large steam roller, a snow plough and some other wonderful giants. Sometimes after school, when the yard went quiet, me and my friends would climb through the fence and play on these things pretending to drive them, they had loads of wheels and levers to pull and turn. It was great fun. Over the fence at the end of our back garden were two fields where Farmer Howard used to keep cows. There was an avenue of horse chestnut trees where we could get across the field without the cows chasing us, though Mr Howard did. He had bandy legs and would shout and wave his stick at us, but we always made it to the safety of the gravel pits or back home again. I think he was pretty harmless really, and he never stopped us from picking blackberries in the hedges – that was, if the O'Dells had left any behind.

Roger Clarke

Buckinghamshire

Dorney, The Church
c1955 D87028

Our 'beach' at old Bletchley

Back in the 1950s, us locals of 'old' Bletchley (which has now been absorbed into Milton Keynes) had a real 'inland seaside', it was great. We used to swim there or just walk across to a lovely clean 'beach', and wherever you dug there was almost pure white sand. Where was it? Beacon Lake, an old flooded gravel pit. The only thing that wasn't very nice was that we had to get changed in amongst the bushes, but most of them were gorse bushes, and they were very prickly. We couldn't go to the end part (where the Argos store is now, on the Beacon Retail Park in Watling Street) because it was thick clay underfoot, and was overgrown with bulrushes, and it was really cold water. Down the main big part of the lake was also dangerous because it was really deep (some older people used to swim right out, but only if they were strong swimmers, because they used to say it was sometimes a bit scary because of a 'pull' in the currents) and in places the water was very cold, but yes, it was our real piece of inland seaside, and we had many, many happy hours there. We all went there mainly together, in a group, and the older people always looked out for the younger ones. We were mainly from the Western Road and suchlike areas. It was safe then, parents never had any cause to worry about their children, not like today! It must have looked weird for anyone driving down the old A5 to see us all crossing the road with big black blown-up inner tubes over our shoulders – we'd be crossing over to where TK Maxx is now, that site used to be a brush factory called 'Beacon Brushes'. I don't think anyone is allowed to swim in the lake now, it's so very deep. But us 'old locals' used to have lovely times there in those days, although it all seems a long time ago now. *Margaret Hogg (née Margaret McCracken)*

Picking wild violets

When I was a child in the 1950s my friend Jean and I used to pick wild violets in the wood just along the towpath on the right hand side of this photograph of Dorney, in South Buckinghamshire. The wood was a carpet of yellow celandines in spring and the scent from the wild violets was reward in itself. We lived in Dorney Reach so most of our childhood was spent by the River Thames.

Monica Peck

> " We used to pick wild violets in the wood on the right hand side of this photograph of Dorney."

Dorney, The Reach 1951 D87007

Rolling Easter eggs down West Wycombe Hill

These are some of my memories from my childhood living at High Wycombe in the 1950s. My family lived on Abercrombie Avenue for a while and I remember playing with spinning tops and a whip in the street with groups of kids. There was a woodyard there, and when it closed we used to climb in and play hide and seek all over the piles of wood. On Saturday mornings we would go to a cartoon matinee at The Grand cinema on Desborough Road. I also recall playing with 'conkers', and rolling Easter eggs down the hill above West Wycombe, near the church on the hill with the Golden Ball on top of its tower. The Wycombe area was a great place to grow up.

Maureen Ingram

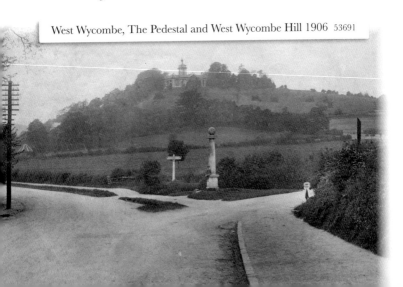

West Wycombe, The Pedestal and West Wycombe Hill 1906 53691

Childhood memories of the village pond

"I spent many hours catching sticklebacks in the pond."

When we were young in the 1930s my friends and I spent many hours catching sticklebacks in the pond at Chalfont St Giles. A fishing net cost tuppence in those days which was regarded as a lot of money, but it was worth every penny!

William Taylor

Chalfont St Giles, The Village and the Pond c1965   C498043

My childhood in Marlow

Marlow, From the Lock
1901 47125

I grew up in Marlow during the 1960s. I have wonderful memories of a really free childhood of bike rides, exploring the woods, rowing a very old boat on the river, even swimming in the river (which my mum never found out about), and just general messing about! We used to go to Marlow Common and play in the trenches, or trek through the woods to Marlow Bottom to make camps, or go down to the end of St Peter's Street to fish. On weekends and holidays we would be out all day. When I go back for a visit I am amazed at how far and wide we kids used to wander! I remember going to see the Beatles' film 'A Hard Days Night' at the Regal, it was fantastic! If there was cricket on we would go and watch with my dad playing and have a picnic. Marlow is still a lovely town and I especially love the swans and walking by the river of a summer's evening.

Miss M

Aunty Eliza and her son Alf

My Great Aunty Eliza lived in an area of Buckland (near Aylesbury) called Buckland Wharf, in a long, low, white bungalow where time seemed to stand still except that the grandfather clock ticked in her parlour to tell us otherwise. The room was very dark because the blinds were drawn "to keep out the sun". There was a heavily framed picture of her husband on the wall – a severe looking man with a handlebar moustache, who seemed very much the Victorian gentleman. I cannot remember the furniture in her bungalow but I vividly remember the rag rugs on the floor. In her kitchen she cooked over a range, did her washing in an old butler sink and bathed weekly in an old tin bath. She was quite the handywoman and on her 80th birthday she very proudly showed off her latest creation – a bright emerald green knitted petticoat (my cousin and I were told off for having a fit of the giggles when we saw it).

My mother and her cousin Bill would always holiday with Aunty Eliza when they were little. One memorable day they had dressed her "chuckens" who seriously protested about their treatment and were flying round the parlour in a highly agitated fashion. Poor Eliza hated birds and nearly had the vapours, and cried: "You wretched children, git them chucks out of my best parlour right now!" Mum and Bill only had bread and dripping for their supper that night as a punishment.

Aunt Eliza' son Alf lived over the road. He more or less lived in his shed, which was his workroom. On one visit we tried to winkle him out of his shed and noticed the sign on the door: 'The man wot lends his tools is out.' So we never asked him for anything! On another visit we saw this sign: 'Plant for hire – hammer 1p, spade 1p – knock for details.' Family legend had it that Alf never took his cap off and even wore it in bed.

Christine Beddows

Gran Honour of Oakley

I recall as a boy living in Thame Road at Oakley in the 1950s having to pass the church at dusk, having been in the village playing field until late. We had an old lady who had lived next to us, a Mrs Honour, who we called Gran Honour, who had died and was buried just inside the gate of the churchyard. On passing the graveyard in the dark I would call "Goodnight Gran" and run past as fast as I could for fear she might rise up and chase me.

Eric Brooks

> "On passing the graveyard in the dark I would call "Goodnight Gran."

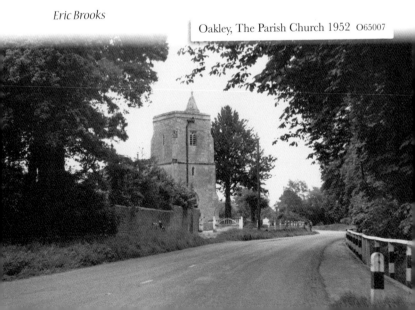

Oakley, The Parish Church 1952 O65007

"All Clear" at the Post Office

I was born in a cottage opposite the Wheatsheaf pub at Maids Morton. It was still a very pretty old village in my youth, and I have happy memories of growing up there. I remember Baroness Kinloss, relative to the Duke of Buckingham, dressed all in black, knocking on our door to wait until there were no customers in Mrs Roberts' Post Office. I would be dispatched to the Post Office and run back to our house with the "All Clear". After the Baroness died, her house in the middle of the village was pulled down to make way for the new housing estate that stretched right down the length of the village, taking in Culley's farm also.

Carole Orpe (née Smith)

Maids Moreton, The Post Office c1955   M264010

My favourite bridge

I remember this bridge at Denham from when I was little and living in Higher Denham. We often walked into the village this way, past the lovely brick wall and past the hut where we got free orange juice after the war. My grandmother ran The Plough pub which was up the road straight ahead in the photo. My brother once fell in the river near this bridge. We were in the tiny newsagent's shop in the village, and he went out the back door and fell into the river. It wasn't deep and he was soon fished out, but we still tease him about it! I took my children back to Denham (from Canada) a few years ago, and the same lady was still running that tiny newsagent's shop. She seemed old when I was a child and must have been well into her 80s by the time we went back. I had been telling my children about her before we entered, and how she always told us to "Shut that door behind you" before we had got through it. Imagine my surprise when I opened the door and heard that same voice tell me to "Shut that door behind you!". How we all laughed when we left!   *Jennifer Schinkel*

Denham, The Village c1965   D183019

I was evacuated to Princes Risborough

I was evacuated to Princes Risborough from London during the Second World War, together with my mother and aunt and my cousin Roger. Our 'home' was with a lady whose husband was in the army – I called her 'Auntie Nellie', and she was a kind and homely woman. There were three boys in her family and an only daughter, Janet, and my cousin Roger and I went to school with the other children. It was a nice big house with an orchard and a pretty garden, fairly near a railway line. One game that

"We were always hungry during the war, because of the food rationing!"

we children played was putting pennies on the railway track, hiding, and then when the train passed we picked up the coins which were now twice their original size. This now seems a very silly thing to do, but we had no fear at that age. We also made fires, and twisted dough round twigs to cook over the flames, which tasted really good. We were always hungry during the war, because of the food rationing! Food was scarce, and we all had ration cards. One of the highlights of our stay with Auntie Nellie was the weekly dance at the WI Hall. We all went – the children danced as well, and as there were no men around, women partnered women. I remember hot sunny days, filled with happy times with lovely people, and the war seemed not to touch us.

Billie Gwilliam (now Billie Willcocks)

One of my boots is in Banks Pond at Haddenham!

In 1944 me and my two brothers were evacuated to Haddenham, and it was one of the best years of my childhood. We lived with an old couple named Mr and Mrs Saw in a house, I think it was named Dolly Cote House and was next to a farm. This was a long time ago now, but one thing I know is that one of my boots is in Banks Pond in the village, as one of my brothers threw it in there. If Banks Pond has not been drained it has been in there ever since!

Len Friday

Haddenham, Church End Green 1951 H375006

Medmenham during the war

I was born in 1942 and my first memories are of the Dog and Badger pub in Medmenham, near Marlow, where I lived for six years following my birth, with my mother and my grandparents, John and Lillian Nye. During the war a couple of bombs fell on the village, one damaged the Post Office, next to the Dog and Badger, and the other ruined Mr Jones's new house which he'd moved to from London to escape the Blitz! I was told that Grandpa had constructed an Anderson shelter in the garden of the pub, but when the bombers came over we had to shelter in the cellar because the Anderson shelter housed black market petrol! A bend in the Thames by Medmenham, apparently, was an excellent guide to the German bombers bound for Coventry, particularly by moonlight.

> "When the bombers came over we had to shelter in the cellar because the Anderson Shelter housed black market petrol!"

'Poppital'

The Wendover Spitfire

I spent part of the war in Wendover as an evacuee from the bombing of London. I recall a huge 'thermometer' that was erected on the clock tower at Wendover as part of the local fundraising drive to pay for a Spitfire, it was graduated in pounds sterling with a picture of a Spitfire at the top. We children, and of course the rest of the Wendover community, subscribed as much as we could, as often as we could, in order to purchase our very own Spitfire, as Wendover's contribution to the war effort.

Edward (Ted) Pace

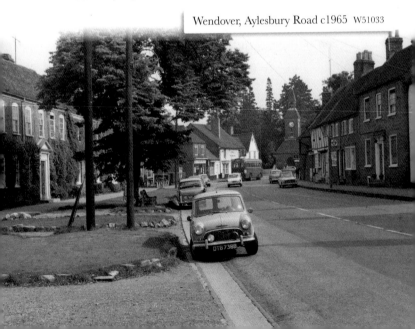

Wendover, Aylesbury Road c1965 W51033

Memories of Wendover C of E school in the 1950s

I went to Wendover Primary School in the 1950s, when it was situated beside the clock tower seen in the distance of photograph W51033 on the opposite page. The headmaster was then Mr H J Figg Edgington, who wore his cap and gown always. I had the best time there. We would walk the Heron Path on nature walks, going down through the recreation ground towards the church and pond, and then back past the stream which had sticklebacks and red throats in it. We did country dancing in the school hall, '123 Hop to the Polka' and so on, and we'd also sit cross-legged on the floor there and listen to records and stories played on a wooden record player. I first read 'Alice in Wonderland' there and Mr Edginton made us promise to read the book again when we grew up – I remembered that much later in my life and purchased two beautifully illustrated copies to share with my grandchildren. The boys would play football at break time and the girls would swing on the climbing frame. There was a big hand bell which had to be rung at break times and we took turns to be bell monitor. We had to go out a few minutes before time and watch the big hands of the clock on the clock tower clunk into place before running around the playgrounds ringing the bell with all our might. It was a very special place.

Glenys Houghton

Oh, when sweets came off ration at last!

I lived in Fenny Stratford as a child in the 1950s. A particular memory I have of those days is of Leeson's shop opposite the cinema on Watling Street, it was the first shop that I ever bought anything in. It was when sweets had just come off ration (wartime rationing on sugar and sweets did not end until February 1953) and my mother gave both my sister and I two pence and we walked to the shop where Mr Leeson gave us each a bag with a mixture of small goodies in. It was absolute heaven to us, who had never had shop-bought sweets before.

Roger Clarke

RAF 90 Group Medmenham

After joining the RAF as aircrew in 1950 and being re-mustered as motor mechanic in 1951, I was posted to RAF Medmenham in 1952 where I was attached to the motor pool. It was a wonderful posting. I have fond memories of my time there, including walking along the river banks and drinking at the Dog and Badger pub in Medmenham village – on pay night, eagerly going down the road from the camp to the Dog and Badger was easy, but coming back up the hill with a few pints aboard was the hard part! I also remember on one occasion trying to visit every pub in Marlow and drinking half a pint at each one – I failed!

Happy memories!

Bob Neil

My idyllic time in Buckinghamshire as a child

In 1954 my army father was posted to the staff college (JSSC) at Latimer in Buckinghamshire after his three years in the Korean war. One of the happier parts of my childhood was spent in a lovely little rented cottage adjoining a farm with a big barn where we could play, and there were chickens and horses for us to enjoy. I think it was on the road out of Chesham. The school I went to was called Long Meadow. We often went to Chesham to feed the ducks, and I also remember visiting the model village at Beaconsfield and going shopping in Amersham. It was a safe and stress-free time for my family, especially after my dad's two years spent as a prisoner of war. Sadly, we soon had to move on to the next place…and then the next…as constant upheaval and change was the norm for us army kids. But I always remember the idyllic time we spent in Buckinghamshire. Lovely memories.

Alison Fowles

Beaconsfield, Bekonscot Model Village c1960   B609123

Memories of Aylesbury in the 1960s & 70s

I have many happy memories of growing up in Aylesbury in the 1960s and 1970s, when it seemed to be a bustling busy town with many little shops. These shops included Weatherhead's book shop in Kingsbury Square (where I loved spending hours looking at the second-hand 10p books in old boxes underneath the tables!) and Baker's toy shop in Buckingham Street, which I would visit with my dad – sometimes he would treat me to some of the little plastic animals that were displayed in a glass case at the far end of the shop, for my farmyard. I also used to visit the 'Pages of Aylesbury' bread shop (also in Buckingham Street) with my mum for our bread and I remember looking longingly at all their cakes displayed in the window.

A big memory I have of living in Aylesbury in the 1960s and 70s was the annual Carnival which we would always watch from the top of Buckingham Road. I remember it being quite a big celebration, with marching bands and a procession of large lorries greatly decorated by the individual clubs, and all the people waving and cheering like mad. We would then follow the procession into town, where the streets were crowded with people, ending up at the Market Square. We'd then visit the Fair through the archway, which was held on the field by the Cattle Market, later to be the site for the Civic Centre. I also remember the 'Hobble on the Cobbles', with loud music and dancing in the evening...but I was always too young to attend!

Vicky Williams

Aylesbury, Market Square c1955   A84050

Winch gliding with my father

My father, Edward Wyatt, spent every spare moment he could flying his glider at Denham airfield in the 1950s. We lived in Higher Denham, and as young children my brother, sister and I were taken to the airfield on many a Sunday. We were strapped into the back seat of the glider and off we would go. I remember the winch letting go, and then we soared up to what seemed like the heavens. Once we were up, my father often insisted that we take the controls. My dad also had a small plane, and would take us flying to high altitudes to help alleviate whooping cough (I think). We looped the loop, and felt sure we would fall out of the open cockpit...fond memories! We moved to Canada in 1955, but when my dad passed away in 1983 he requested that he be buried in Denham churchyard. This was where his heart was always, particularly the airfield...

Jennifer Schinkel (née Wyatt)

Denham, The Airfield c1965   D183014

The canal bank down from Park Street bridge

When I was young in the 1950s the opposite bank of the Grand Union Canal as seen in the 1897 photograph 39642 (below) was the site of Frith's, the builders' supply company. My father was a salesman for them for many years. The location was called Hilda's Wharf, and in the 1940s and early 1950s some of Frith's supplies such as bathroom tiles were delivered there by narrow boat – tiles are fragile and the canal was a smooth ride. Of course Frith's is long gone, and a row of townhouses now stands on its site.

Doug Caton

Aylesbury, The Canal 1897 39642

My father was the manager of the Bull's Head Hotel at Aylesbury

My father was the manager of the Bull's Head Hotel at Aylesbury in the 1950s, Mr Ronald F Williams. I remember when the Italian film star Sophia Loren was staying at the hotel and she joined us for tea as my mother is Italian also, they had a good long chat. How lovely to see this fantastic old hotel again and what a shame it's no longer there – demolished in 1969, the hotel's former site is now the entry to the Hale Leys shopping centre.

Shirley Williams

and so was mine...

My father, Bill Thomas, was one of the last managers of the Bull's Head Hotel at Aylesbury. He helped the police when they stayed at the hotel working on the Great Train Robbery of 1963.

Hedley Thomas

Aylesbury, The Bull's Head Hotel c1965 A84082

I was a pre-student and nurse at this hospital

I worked at the Canadian Red Cross Memorial Hospital at Taplow from 1954 to 1958.

I lived in the old Isolation Hospital at Cippenham that had been converted to a nurses' home, and we travelled by bus from there to The Canadian. The hospital was always very busy, although had no A & E. We always seemed to be short-staffed and we had to turn our hand to everything. Working hours were 7.00am till 1.00pm or 4.00pm till 10.00pm, nights was from 10.00pm till 7.00am. We nurses wore a very smart uniform, a royal blue dress, a starched white apron, a white hat and brown flat shoes.

> "We nurses wore a very smart uniform, a royal blue dress, a starched white apron, a white hat and brown flat shoes."

My first ward was the Rheumatic Fever Unit for children. The only visiting hours were on Sunday, from 2.00pm till 4.00pm, which was so hard for the little ones. I worked on all the Wards 1 to 13. Wards 12 and 13 were for TB patients and 1 and 2 for the Rheumatic Fever. If you were on night duty you were given two Wards to work, and I frequently had this job. It was a long walk from Wards 1, 2, and 3 to 12 and 13 (some people said it was a quarter of a mile from one end to the other) and NO RUNNING was allowed! Whilst I was working on the TB unit, Richard Todd, the actor, came to visit and he signed my apron! Sadly I had to send it to the wash, as was expected of us. This was probably akin to washing Brad Pitt's autograph away nowadays!

Valerie Kent

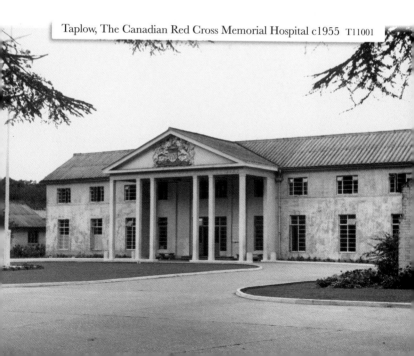

Taplow, The Canadian Red Cross Memorial Hospital c1955   T11001

Meeting my dad out of the Wolverton Works

This photograph from around 1910 shows crowds of men leaving the Wolverton railway works. When I was young in the 1950s, I used to cycle to Wolverton every Friday to meet my dad when he came out of the railway carriage works at the end of the day. When the hooter went, about five thousand men came out the gates. Dad used to buy me sweets from Musket's sweet shop and take me to the indoor market, and we'd have a cup of tea at Ethel's, she ran the tea bar. Then we'd cycle back to Loughton.

Jose Mabbutt

Wolverton, Stratford Road, Men leaving the Wolverton Works c1910 W176501

I did a job here on my first day at work

I can never pass through Maids Moreton without recalling my first day at work as an apprentice electrician for The East Midlands Electricity Board, Buckingham. It was April 14th 1958 and I was assigned to Mr Jack Holland, electrician, and we were sent to install a lighting point in a rear toilet for 'Mrs Holmes, The Old Bakehouse, Main Street', and I have never forgotten it. It was the beginning of a career in the electrical business that lasted until I retired in 2003, having completed over 45 years in the trade. I can never forget that address nor the gentleman, now sadly gone, who gave me my first start on that long 'electrical road'. Thank you, Jack.

"Thank you, Jack."

Rick Brock

Maids Moreton, The Village c1955   M264006

Life at The Stores, Chaloners Hill, Steeple Claydon

I was seven when my family moved to Steeple Claydon from London in 1956. We lived at number 1 Chaloners Hill, otherwise known as The Stores, which my parents ran until the late 1960s. In this photograph the petrol pumps outside The Stores are just visible on the left-hand-side of the road. Steeple Claydon was a wonderful place to grow up. I have happy memories of the village school, the meandering stream that ran just outside the village known as 'the planks', long walks down the Calvert road, and making children's camps that were hidden away in quiet corners. Then there were cricket matches down the recreation ground on summer Sunday afternoons and rowdy football matches on autumn Saturdays, dances at the Library hall (which were always followed by a fight!), church on Sunday for some, chapel for others, and the public bar of the village pubs for the majority.

Across the road from us Vic Burrows ran the bakery and we were treated to the smell of freshly baked bread every morning. Mrs Whiting had the newsagent's and Cyril and Ruby Griffin ran the Fountain pub. There were five pubs in Steeple Claydon then, whereas poor old Middle Claydon, East Claydon and Botolph Claydon didn't have one between them. We had nine shops in the village in those days, including a Post Office, and they supplied most of our needs.

At Austin's you could buy fishing tackle and a penknife and get a haircut if you wanted one. Dennis Robinson, who also ran the Phoenix pub, would mend your bike and he also displayed the latest Raleigh bike in his workshop window. This was torture for us boys – we would gaze at it for hours, making ambitious plans to raise the ten or twelve pounds required to buy it. We vowed to get jobs on the local farms or, when the season came, spend the summer evenings fruit picking at Claydon House. We went fruit picking but five shillings at the end of the week was a long way short of ten pounds and it burnt a hole in our pockets and was soon spent.

Paul Curtis

Steeple Claydon c1955 S565008

The best roast lunches ever, at The Swan in West Wycombe

I worked in High Wycombe in the 1970s as a young man in my twenties and discovered The Swan pub at West Wycombe (you can see its sign on the right-hand side of this pic). Every weekday lunchtime they did a roast dinner and pudding and a coffee for a set price. There was no other menu. I remember the dining room having some big and some small tables. The same people went there for lunch every day, but because I had only been going there two days a week for two years, no-one actually spoke to me yet! The most fantastic roast lunches were served up by two old ladies and a daughter of one of them, I think. I would guess the daughter to be forty and the other ladies to be ancient. It was like school dinners on steroids. Sometimes tourists would call in and you would see them looking for a menu, saying something like "Perhaps a little salad, darling, or some tuna on brown bread?". Suddenly roast lamb and three veg would clatter onto the table in front of them, and they would always be too scared of the old ladies to say anything.

Donald Macdonald

> "It was like school dinners on steroids."

West Wycombe, High Street 1954 W340016

Shopping in Hazlemere in the 1950s and 60s

I was born in Hazlemere (near High Wycombe) in 1953 and grew up there. Hazlemere had a good choice of shops when I was young, including the Post Office and newsagent's, a record shop, a boutique called 'Maggie Mae', a furniture shop, a chemist's, a sweet and toy shop (Duggin's) and a general stores amongst them. There were lots of people about and the shops were always busy. We did all our food shopping in Hazlemere and only went to nearby High Wycombe for other things, where there were bigger stores like Woolworth and Murrays.

From a very early age my mother used to send me to the crossroads to do the shopping for her. Every Friday after school I used to go to Ford's the grocer's with my shopping list for the week, order all the goods, pay for them and then walk back via the sweet shop to spend the 3d (that's about 1p in decimal money) that my mum gave me. Ford's had a grey van which was used to deliver the goods to our house. Often the shopping arrived home before me! Hazlemere crossroads wasn't that busy with traffic then and sometimes I'd go up there on my scooter or bike with no worries.

Gill Pateman (née Blake)

The most interesting barber's shop in the world

Probably just behind the photographer in this view of the crossroads at Hazlemere (H470010) was an old-fashioned men's barber shop. All the old men would go there for a haircut and mums would take their sons too. What the mums never knew is that when you sat in the alcove to have your hair washed, there were numerous naughty pictures that could only be seen from in there. I wonder if any boy ever told his mum what he'd seen?

Donald Macdonald

Hazlemere, The Crossroads c1960 H470010

Market day in Buckingham

My father was a drover who worked at the cattle market in Buckingham until it closed in the 1950s. His name was Reg Coulton ('Ginger'). I also remember that poultry was sold in a yard further down the street. We kept warm in the winter in the 'Baron's Grill'. Happy days.

Rod Coulton

Buckingham, Town Hall and Market Place c1950 B280027

Buckingham, High Street and Cattle Market c1950 B280022

Catching newts at Tylers Green

The building in the background to the right of this photograph with the little spire was my school when I was 11 in 1966. I spent many hours catching newts in that pond in the foreground.
It was partly surrounded by a brick and concrete wall and the newts would tuck themselves into little caves.

Donald Macdonald

> "I spent many hours catching newts in that pond."

Tylers Green, The Green c1955   T354005

My school days at Farnham Common

I remember walking from Hedgerley to the school at Farnham Common in the winter of 1971, only to arrive at the gates and see this view but with the whole car park and playground being flooded. No school today! Sometimes when there was flooding it was a couple of days before the water had drained away. On the left of this photograph is where we used to stand waiting for the door to open for our school disco etc. It was a great school. Teachers I particularly remember were Miss Painter and Mrs Benjamin – she was a great teacher, but unfortunately I never did get the hang of needlework in her lessons!

Pete Cronin

Farnham Common, The County Primary School c1965   F196013

The dinners at Farnham Common school

I started at the primary school at Farnham Common in 1970, I still think it was the best school ever. School dinners – OMG! We sat on tables of (I think) 8 and at the end of each table we had servers who went up and got our lunch for us, in those days you were allowed seconds as well! Then every week the seating order changed and everyone moved up a seat to be a server. Things I remember having for school dinners were Spam fritters, chocolate sponge and pink custard, apple and cornflake tart, very green or very white cabbage, and gravy! And there was always fish on Fridays. We always had knives, folks and spoons on the tables and ate off proper plates, not the plastic tray things that children have nowadays. I can also remember being selected to go and do the teachers' washing up after break or lunchtime and eating the biscuits that were left over – no child is allowed anywhere near a staff room these days.

> "Spam fritters, chocolate sponge and pink custard, apple and cornflake tart, very green or very white cabbage, and gravy!"

Sue Bojczuk (née Hailes)

Watching the building of the M1 Motorway on the way to school

As a youngster in the 1950s and 1960s I grew up just outside Newport Pagnell at Tongwell Farm. I well remember the announcement in 1967 that they were going to build a new city called Milton Keynes and the farm would be part of that new city, but before that happened living on Tongwell Farm was a great deal of fun for me and I always had plenty of things to occupy my time. I attended school in Newport Pagnell and usually got there on my bike and went to my grandmother's house (Kate Daniells) in number 34 Spring Gardens. I then left the bike at her house and walked the two hundred yards to the school. With the building of the M1 Motorway (the first section opened in 1959) the access to the road into town was cut off and the main contractors, Laing's, used to ferry us pupils in a minibus both to school and back again in the evening. As a youngster, seeing the road project grow was most exciting, as were the huge Euclids which were the primary machines used for scraping away and levelling the ground.

Bob Anderson

> "I well remember the announcement in 1967 that they were going to build a new city called Milton Keynes."

Starstruck at Bletchley!

In 1963 when I was 15 I left Bletchley Road Secondary Modern School, and went to work at Moss's in Fenny Stratford. I thought it was great to earn £3 a week, I did a lot with that. I used to go to lots of dances each week, there were loads to go to at various venues – there was the Palace (or Palais de Dance) at Wolverton, with dances twice a week, Murlsey village on a Friday, and the Wilton Hall in Bletchley on both Wednesday and Saturday. We had a job deciding where to go, it was mainly the Wilton Hall that won, because it was in walking distance from home and so there were no fares to pay out for. We used to regularly see the Hollies, the Searchers, Gerry and the Pacemakers, Brian Poole and the Tremeloes, the Animals, even Lulu, she did her debut gig there. They were great days. Yes, there was a bit of trouble some weeks, but nothing major like today's youths get up to. Loads of 'big-ish' name groups played in Bletchley, people came from miles away to see these bands. It was chaos when the Rolling Stones came there. I used to have to work till nearly 6 o'clock on a Saturday evening so I couldn't have got anywhere near the Wilton Hall to queue up to see them, BUT I did get a quick glance at the Stones on my way home from work, they were sitting in the Mokaris café eating beans on toast – well, they were no different from most people, were they!

Margaret Hogg (née McCracken)

Haircuts at Sherington

Just before the 1960s transformed our innocent lives, us village boys at Sherington had a limited choice of tonsorial art; indeed you could count the number of available haircuts (styles wasn't a word used for men or boys) on the fingers of one hand: Short Back & Sides, Square Neck, Feather Neck and Crew Cut. The deed was done by Uncle Ben, who cut hair on a regular basis as well as doing his main job as the village carpenter and handyman. He held court in the kitchen of his cottage, where he had all the gear… a big chair with a boy box to raise you up to men's height, mirrors to look at yourself whilst he cut away, waiting chairs, magazines or comics, Brylcream and 'Tonic', which smelled of ladies' perfume and which was only applied to men upon request.

Short Back & Sides was the standard cut for 90% of the male population at that time. It left only the crown hair, the length of which to be individually determined, either long, medium or short, and a finishing touch of Brylcream for the men was a must to spruce them up. Square Neck and Feather Neck were pretty much the same thing, with the finish at the nape of the neck being either squared across with the clippers or feathered. The Square Neck was a Teddy Boy cut – Elvis was the role model, so the top was usually long and quiffed. With both these styles the biggest difference from the Short Back & Sides was the tight hairline around your ears. Crew Cuts were about, but were really a 'Yankee' thing and were few and far between in Sherington. The only bloke I knew in the village with one was Slick Slater.

Eventually we grew up enough to get our hair styled in Newport Pagnell, just in time for the Beatles to hit the scene – and then we all wanted mop-top haircuts, just like the Fab Four.

Alan Garratt

This is me when I was a lad!

The lad leaning on the wall in this photograph was John Cook, whose father was a policeman in Newport Pagnell, the guy to the left in the dark suite is me, and the lad sitting on the pillar (to the right) was David Ashworth, son of Major Ashworth, who lived in Silver Street.

Anthony Burt

Newport Pagnell, North Bridge from the Play Pen 1956 N62050

A little book of memories

I lived here for the first 25 years of my life

I lived at the house just at the top of this photograph from my birth in 1944 until I was 25 years old. The outbuildings can clearly be seen in the adjoining field to the family home. I spent all my childhood years playing with my brother and friends here. I used to love watching the working barges going through the locks. My grandfather kept The Three Locks (known then as The New Inn) as its publican for 16 years, in the days when the barges were horse-drawn.

Stephanie Mcpherson

Stoke Hammond, The Three Locks c1965 S566012b

The people in this photo...

This photograph of the Cornmarket in High Wycombe pictures my father-in-law, Guilford Emery (now deceased), his daughter Jen (now deceased), and one of his sons, my brother-in-law David Emery. We first discovered the photograph in what used to be the Safeways supermarket (now Morrisons) in High Wycombe, where a framed copy of it hangs on their wall by the checkouts. I had shopped there but never noticed it until another local spotted the family. We have had lots of discussions about the picture and where the remaining members of the family were when it was taken. I purchased a printed copy of it from The Francis Frith Collection and it hangs on our wall, where it always sets up a talking point.

Mrs Maureen Emery

High Wycombe, Cornmarket 1951 H84064

FRANCIS FRITH

PIONEER   VICTORIAN   PHOTOGRAPHER

Francis Frith, founder of the world-famous photographic archive, was a complex and multi-talented man. A devout Quaker and a highly successful Victorian businessman, he was philosophical by nature and pioneering in outlook. By 1855 he had already established a wholesale grocery business in Liverpool, and sold it for the astonishing sum of £200,000, which is the equivalent today of over £15,000,000. Now in his thirties, and captivated by the new science of photography, Frith set out on a series of pioneering journeys up the Nile and to the Near East.

INTRIGUE AND EXPLORATION

He was the first photographer to venture beyond the sixth cataract of the Nile. Africa was still the mysterious 'Dark Continent', and Stanley and Livingstone's historic meeting was a decade into the future. The conditions for picture taking confound belief. He laboured for hours in his wicker dark-room in the sweltering heat of the desert, while the volatile chemicals fizzed dangerously in their trays. Back in London he exhibited his photographs and was 'rapturously cheered' by members of the Royal Society. His reputation as a photographer was made overnight.

VENTURE OF A LIFE-TIME

By the 1870s the railways had threaded their way across the country, and Bank Holidays and half-day Saturdays had been made obligatory by Act of Parliament. All of a sudden the working man and his family were able to enjoy days out, take holidays, and see a little more of the world.

With typical business acumen, Francis Frith foresaw that these new tourists would enjoy having souvenirs to commemorate their days out. For the next thirty years he travelled the country by train and by pony and trap, producing fine photographs of seaside resorts and beauty spots that were keenly bought by millions of Victorians. These prints were painstakingly pasted into family albums and pored over during the dark nights of winter, rekindling precious memories of summer excursions. Frith's studio was soon supplying retail shops all over the country, and by 1890 F Frith & Co had become the greatest specialist photographic publishing company in the world, with over 2,000 sales outlets, and pioneered the picture postcard.

FRANCIS FRITH'S LEGACY

Francis Frith had died in 1898 at his villa in Cannes, his great project still growing. By 1970 the archive he created contained over a third of a million pictures showing 7,000 British towns and villages.

Frith's legacy to us today is of immense significance and value, for the magnificent archive of evocative photographs he created provides a unique record of change in the cities, towns and villages throughout Britain over a century and more. Frith and his fellow studio photographers revisited locations many times down the years to update their views, compiling for us an enthralling and colourful pageant of British life and character.

We are fortunate that Frith was dedicated to recording the minutiae of everyday life. For it is this sheer wealth of visual data, the painstaking chronicle of changes in dress, transport, street layouts, buildings, housing and landscape that captivates us so much today, offering us a powerful link with the past and with the lives of our ancestors.

Computers have now made it possible for Frith's many thousands of images to be accessed almost instantly. The archive offers every one of us an opportunity to examine the places where we and our families have lived and worked down the years. Its images, depicting our shared past, are now bringing pleasure and enlightenment to millions around the world a century and more after his death.

For further information visit: www.francisfrith.com

INTERIOR DECORATION

Frith's photographs can be seen framed and as giant wall murals in thousands of pubs, restaurants, hotels, banks, retail stores and other public buildings throughout Britain. These provide interesting and attractive décor, generating strong local interest and acting as a powerful reminder of gentler days in our increasingly busy and frenetic world.

FRITH PRODUCTS

All Frith photographs are available as prints and posters in a variety of different sizes and styles. In the UK we also offer a range of other gift and stationery products illustrated with Frith photographs, although many of these are not available for delivery outside the UK – see our web site for more information on the products available for delivery in your country.

THE INTERNET

Over 100,000 photographs of Britain can be viewed and purchased on the Frith web site. The web site also includes memories and reminiscences contributed by our customers, who have personal knowledge of localities and of the people and properties depicted in Frith photographs. If you wish to learn more about a specific town or village you may find these reminiscences fascinating to browse. Why not add your own comments if you think they would be of interest to others? See **www.francisfrith.com**

PLEASE HELP US BRING FRITH'S PHOTOGRAPHS TO LIFE

Our authors do their best to recount the history of the places they write about. They give insights into how particular towns and villages developed, they describe the architecture of streets and buildings, and they discuss the lives of famous people who lived there. But however knowledgeable our authors are, the story they tell is necessarily incomplete.

Frith's photographs are so much more than plain historical documents. They are living proofs of the flow of human life down the generations. They show real people at real moments in history; and each of those people is the son or daughter of someone, the brother or sister, aunt or uncle, grandfather or grandmother of someone else. All of them lived, worked and played in the streets depicted in Frith's photographs.

We would be grateful if you would give us your insights into the places shown in our photographs: the streets and buildings, the shops, businesses and industries. Post your memories of life in those streets on the Frith website: what it was like growing up there, who ran the local shop and what shopping was like years ago; if your workplace is shown tell us about your working day and what the building is used for now. Read other visitors' memories and reconnect with your shared local history and heritage. With your help more and more Frith photographs can be brought to life, and vital memories preserved for posterity, and for the benefit of historians in the future.

Wherever possible, we will try to include some of your comments in future editions of our books. Moreover, if you spot errors in dates, titles or other facts, please let us know, because our archive records are not always completely accurate—they rely on 140 years of human endeavour and hand-compiled records. You can email us using the contact form on the website.

Thank you!

For further information, trade, or author enquiries
please contact us at the address below:

**The Francis Frith Collection, 6 Oakley Business Park,
Wylye Road, Dinton, Wiltshire SP3 5EU.**

Tel: +44 (0)1722 716 376 Fax: +44 (0)1722 716 881
e-mail: sales@francisfrith.co.uk **www.francisfrith.com**